Island Song

Written and illustrated by Nadine Cowan

Collins

Cadence was named after music's rhythm and flow,
and into her name she's begun to grow.

She's grown to love the melody of sound,
and has come to know that music is all around.

From high up in the sky where the planes whizz by,
To the tops of the trees where the parrots fly.

From fun days at the beach
to the kitchen with granny,
Cadence hears music from every nook and cranny.

Grandpa loves calypso,
    So much so …

That when Cadence was born, he said,
    "Name her Calypso!"
To which Mama and Papa said … "NO!"

He sways and rocks to the calypso sound,
Like an energetic pup that's leaping around.
While the old records play, his heart fills with joy,
As memories dance of him as a young boy.

Granny loves jazz ...

   ... every morning, she hums and sings,

Along with the radio until the kitchen timer rings.

The spice jars her tambourines

   and the grater a guiro,

She shakes, and grates and stirs it in slow.

6

Cinnamon and nutmeg rejoice down below,
Into the cornmeal porridge they go.

She stirs in the bay leaves, then rests her hand on
her waist,
And beckons Cadence over, to have a little taste.

Mama loves soul.

Whilst canerowing Cadence's hair,

And oiling her scalp with care,

Mama sings into the comb in her hand,

Between braiding Cadence's curls,

strand by strand.

Papa loves reggae music; like sugar it's sweet,
He turns the dial high
    until his feet can feel the beat.
Laughter waltzes in the air
when Papa gives Mama a glance.
He grabs her in closer
and they both begin to dance.

Her sister Cora loves sweet soca music,
and her brother Calvin loves hip-hop but ...

9

Cadence loves the island's rhythm and flow –
It's like the whole world's a deejay,
    spinning tune after tune.
The set starts with the sunrise as the roosters crow
And the music plays
    beyond the rising of the moon.

COCK-A-DOODLE-DOO!

Every morning as she rises with the heat,
Cadence wakes with wonder,
as each day brings a different beat.

11

Like the soft hiss of a shaker, the pan sizzles!
When the dumplings and fish hit the hot oil,
Cadence hums to the percussion
    as the pots and pans boil.

Whether it's tasty soup, or rice and peas
Granny's cooking wafts around the house
    giving noses a tease.

Granny is a music conductor in the kitchen,
stirring this,
turning that,
hobs hiss,
stews simmer.

Don't let it get too hot,
turn the fire down low.
When the wooden spoon hits the iron pot,
Cadence thinks of dancing to the steel pan's flow.

CLANG! CLANG! CLANG!

When she sways with her grandpa, hand in hand,
They jump up and down to the rhythms of the band.

CLANG! CLANG! CLANG!

Seasonings sprinkle down into the pan.
As the metal hits the wood,
Granny sings,
    "That will make the food taste good!"

The tempo speeds up
when Cadence follows Mama into town;
She sings from the top of the hill
as they make their way down.

They pass a neighbour sweeping –
she is quick on her feet –
It's like maracas grooving
to the chicken's CLUCK and goat's BLEAT.

With a rhythm in her step that jams to the island's beat,
Cadence's flip-flops

CLAP! CLAP! CLAP!

down the street.
With each step, her hair takes flight,
Her hair beads

CLICK! and CLACK!

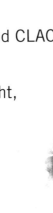

with delight,

As she skips down the hill to catch the bus,
She passes each yard and the dogs bark and fuss.

WOOF! WOOF! WOOF!

Mama smiles, "Look you're starting a procession
And it sounds like they want in on your jam session!"

They climb aboard and Mama pays the fare,
As Cadence swats the singing mosquito from her ear.
The driver turns the music up as they sit down,
Then the wheels speed up as they head into town.

Lots of vendors have come out to trade,
Under their colourful umbrellas
 in the cool of the shade.
Bananas, pineapples and oranges so bright,
Mama holds up a mango and says,
 "This one's just right!"

At the market in the sweltering heat,
gossiping aunts swap stories,
 like chitter chatter on a samba beat,
as they caress fruits looking for
 the perfect one.
Old Man Ivan pushing his snow-cone
 cart under the scorching sun.

CREAK! CREAK! CREAK!

Chiming in with a bell,
He wipes sweat from his brow and lets out a yell,
"I have cherry, blue raspberry and lemon to sell!"
"Mmmm," thinks Cadence, "it tastes so nice"
As she sips her treat of syrup,
    and fine crushed ice.

CHOP! CHOP! CHOP!

Here comes more percussion,
Mixed in with the aunties' discussion.
It's the coconut man, swinging at the coconut's shell,
Edging closer to the flesh.
With one final swing, its water laid bare,
A taste of the tropics, so refreshing and clear.

Music, it's everywhere,

The sound of nature is music to her ear.

Like when Cadence climbs up to the waterfall,

a warm breeze whistles through the trees

and the palm tree leaves

wave hello …

… then sway and dance as though the birds

   are singing Grandpa's beloved calypso.

And when they finally reach the waterfall,
    where Cadence loves to play –
– where the water flows like a parade,
on carnival day.
She dances in its burbles,
as it pours down with a
    CRASH!
Then Calvin jumps in with
a loud WOO HOO!
And a great big SPLASH!

When they catch the ferry from the mainland,
to the neighbouring island,
its motor hums,
like a marching band's drums,
sending vibrations through the sea.
The dolphins jump up with excitement and join
    the melody.
The ferry sways,
from side to side,
dancing along,
with each glide.

At the beach, when sand grains dance beneath
    Cadence's feet,
she hears the shaking of maracas on the island beat,
jamming with the waves
as she races the sea to the shore,
and then runs back towards it
to race again once more.

Calvin and his friends sound like
they're in a drum band,
When they perform their
fancy football tricks on the sand.
What's that sound?
Like the bass of Papa's speaker,
    when he plays reggae …

... It's the fishers coming back,
buckets filled with the catch of the day.
The fishers unload the buckets,
Back and forth they sway
As the sun takes a bow,
and begins to fade away.

The sky looks like watercolours on a canvas,
Brushstrokes of orange, purple and pink,
Dance across the horizon,
As though the song and sky are in sync.

But Cadence's favourite part is at bedtime,
when the rain dances on the roof.
The sound is so soothing,
as the moon and stars shine bright.

And the crickets CHIRP!
and the tree frogs CROAK!
a lullaby,
as the island sings ...
GOODNIGHT!

29

Sounds in Cadence's day

"She shakes, and grates and stirs it in slow."

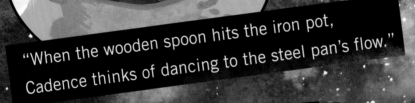

"When the wooden spoon hits the iron pot, Cadence thinks of dancing to the steel pan's flow."

"Papa loves reggae music,
    like sugar it's sweet,
He turns the dial high
    until his feet can feel the beat."

"where the water flows like a parade, on carnival day."

"she hears the shaking of maracas on the island beat, jamming with the waves"

"But Cadence's favourite part is at bedtime, when the rain dances on the roof."

:paw::paw: Ideas for reading :paw::paw:

Written by Jonny Walker
Specialist Teacher and Educational Consultant

Reading session aims

- make links between poems and children's own life experiences
- explore how poets use the senses to describe a scene
- understand how poets use onomatopoeia and rhyme

Spoken language objectives

- ask relevant questions to extend their understanding and knowledge
- use relevant strategies to build their vocabulary
- articulate and justify answers, arguments and opinions
- give well-structured descriptions, explanations and narratives for different purposes, including for expressing feelings

Curriculum links: Geography: Locational knowledge; Music: Appreciate and understand music drawn from different traditions; Understand the history of music

Interest words: calypso, jazz, reggae, soul, soca, hiphop, jam session

Talk before reading

- Look at the cover and read the blurb on the back cover together. Explain that this poem is set on a Caribbean island. Ask children if they can name any Caribbean islands and if they have ever visited the Caribbean themselves.
- Explain that the book explores the girl's favourite sounds around her home. Ask children what sounds make them think of home, and to explain why.
- Ask children if they enjoy music, and what sort of music their family and friends enjoy.

Support personal responses

- Take time to discuss the poem after you have read it. Use the following questions or ask your own.
  - What did you like most about *Island Song*?
  - How does music affect how people feel?
  - Do you prefer being in places that are very noisy or very quiet? Why?
  - What are the different sounds that you hear in your home and your classroom?